# The
# Elegant
# Beast

A Studio Book

The Viking Press

New York

# THE ELEGANT BEAST

*Or, Conversations on*

*Costume, Being a Treatise with Illustrations*

*Showing How Clothes Can Bring Out the*

*Animal in All of Us*

## Leonard Lubin

*To Emilio D'Antuono and Robert Dixon*

First published in 1981 by The Viking Press (A Studio Book)
625 Madison Avenue, New York, N.Y. 10022

Published simultaneously in Canada by
Penguin Books Canada Limited

Library of Congress Cataloging in Publication Data
Lubin, Leonard B
The elegant beast.
(A Studio book)
Summary: Text and illustrations featuring furry and feathered creatures modeling more
than 40 historically accurate garments relate the ebb and flow of fashion over 5 centuries.
1. Costume—History.  [1. Costume—History]  I. Title.
GT511.L8      391′.009      80-52645
ISBN 0-670-29097-1

Printed in Japan by Dai Nippon Printing Co., Ltd., Tokyo

Set in Baskerville

# Contents

**I**t seems to me that certain costumes in the course of Fashion's illustrious history are eminently suited for display on the curvacious silhouettes of animals. Generously padded hippopotamuses, for instance, could easily take the place of the chubby Dutch burghers in the paintings of Frans Hals; and instead of Velázquez's Spanish princesses, with their penchant for the dwarfed grotesque, I envision a pug-nosed Pekinese dressed à la Infanta. If humans can be referred to as eagle-eyed, hawk-nosed, pigeon-toed, leonine, and goatish, or as lame ducks or real dogs, why not outfit our furry, feathered, and scaly chums in clothing that might just show how human they can be?

My very sentiments have already been expressed by the artists Jean Baptiste Oudry and Christophe Huet, in the eighteenth century, and Grandville, in the nineteenth, in their clever illustrations of handsomely dressed animals. Oudry and Huet were partial to monkeys, although they also costumed a variety of other animals in their decorative illustrations; Grandville produced marvelous drawings of fashionably garbed birds and beasts for *Les Animaux*. I salute all three for the inspiration and great amusement that their work provides to this day.

I contend that European Fashion actually began in the Middle Ages, when distinct differences evolved in what men and women wore. Prior to that period, people of both sexes draped upon their forms sheets of fabric that closely resembled bed linens, or they traipsed about in various stages of undress. With the Gothic period, the cut of a garment, its texture and pattern, along with how it was worn, all became important. People discovered how to reveal, and at the same time conceal, the body with optimum style, flair, and ingenuity. These criteria were applied equally to both male and female attire so that each individual could display his or her attributes to their best advantage.

I have tried to touch the high points of each fashionable epoch of history.*With the information provided by an abundance of reference material, I have attempted to depict the distinctive look prevalent in each period. Of course those distinctions are not quite as cut and dried as I would have liked; sometimes the same style overlapped several time periods. People didn't stop wearing a particular article of clothing simply because Louis XVI succeeded Louis XV or because the Middle Ages became the Renaissance. Something else to bear in mind is that the costumes illustrated were worn strictly by the upper strata of society. After all, it was the aristocratic and wealthy who had the time, money, and inclination to be dressed in vogue.

The book concludes with the Belle Epoque. The Great War gave rise to preoccupations of another order. It is my contention also that with the emergence of mass production clothing design lost a good portion of its éclat.

🐾🐾🐾🐾🐾🐾🐾

*The models:* page 9, brown and black rats; page 11, goshawk, white dove, and spotted-billed toucanet; page 13, black rhinoceroses; page 15, Chihuahua and bulldog; page 17, Galápagos tortoise and common toad; page 19, hippopotamus and pygmy hippopotamus; page 21, cocker spaniel and Afghan hound; page 23, Pekinese and vizsla; page 25, African lions; page 27, Eurasian black vulture and lesser sulphur-crested cockatoo; page 29, olive drill and chacma baboon; page 31, Chinese geese; page 33, common domesticated goats; page 35, Chapman's zebras; page 37, llama and camel; page 39, hares; page 41, Siamese cats; page 43, warthog and pig; page 45, ostrich and flamingo; page 47, harbor seal and elephant seal.

🐾🐾🐾🐾🐾🐾🐾

* The dates that appear in the titles for each of the short essays refer to the approximate years during which the style of costume depicted in the plates was most fashionable.

The Burgundian Court of Philip the Good, sage ruler of Flanders, the Low Countries, and most of France, was a rattling arena of style, for nowhere in mid-fifteenth century Western Europe was costume more splendiferous. Under the weighty rule of the Burgundian dukes, including Philip the Good, his father John the Fearless, and those who came before (most of whom were named Philip, with qualifications such as "the Bold," "the Rash," and "the Brave"), industry and trade thrived. Gold poured into the region, as did stunning silks, velvets, and jewels, all of which contributed to the Burgundian predilection for things *de luxe.*

*Those of gentle blood were partial to the* houppelande, *a full and lengthy gown or robe with long trailing sleeves and a high, often turned-down collar. Sleeves were dagged, or "petal scalloped," and edged with fur. The robe was left open from the waist down to facilitate movement, and thus created a dignified train.* Beneath the houppelande noblemen sported a mid-thigh-length doublet or pourpoint, *and masculine calves were sheathed in tight hose attached to the doublet at the waist.* Poulaines, *extremely long and pointed shoes, were curled up at the tips and crowned with tiny bells. In nasty weather these shoes were worn with thick, wooden-soled* pattens, *which were fastened over the instep by a broad band of fabric. The pattens elevated the feet above the mud and muck lest the poulaines be soiled.* The gentleman's head was covered by a chaperon, *a hood arranged in folds which terminated in a long tail, known as a* liripipe. *The liripipe hung down the back or was draped about the shoulders, accompanied by a thickly stuffed* roundlet *or* turban, *open at the top. The excess material at the "head" of the chaperon was petal-scalloped, giving it a cockscomb-like appearance.* Bells were used as trimming on the scalloped sleeves and hood, and often they adorned the baldric, *a belt worn over one shoulder to support a sword.*

*The full-trailing houppelande of a fair lady was held in, high at the waist, by a wide jeweled belt, then allowed to cascade in graceful folds. The long sleeves with scalloped edges were turned back to reveal the lining, which was often of a different color and fabric from the robe itself.* The escoffion, *a thick padded roll of fabric, was worn with a jewel-encrusted net* caul *over a black velvet hood, and sometimes the whole affair was shrouded with a dagged-edged wimple or veil of gauze or silk.* A gold and jeweled necklace about the neck and a pair of fashionable poulaines enclosing the feet completed the "look."

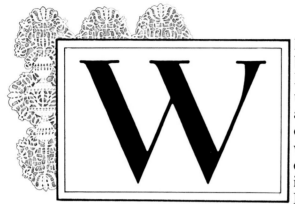

hile knighthood flowered, the bubonic plague raged. Towns and villages were decimated as the plague unleashed its wrath against one and all—good, bad, and undecided. Citizens of every station were crazed with fear and lived each day as if it were their last, as indeed for many of them it was. Despite the fact that clergymen themselves were not exempt from the plague's indelicate touch, the Church boasted a land-office business: everyone turned to religion for security, and the Church became the dominant presence in this bitter time.

The Church provided far more than salvation. Even fashion took its cue from the Gothic architecture of the imposing cathedrals; the spires and pointed arches of the cathedrals were echoed in the elongated slender silhouettes of damsels and their consorts.

*The houppelande still prevailed and, on a masculine frame, was worn either long to the ground or short to the hips. Padded at the shoulders and chest and caught at the waist, it flared into a skirt, sometimes edged with fur. Sleeves were often slit, allowing the arm to protrude and revealing the undertunic. Shoes à la poulaine were still the footwear of the day, and fashionable headgear included the roundlet with chaperon and liripipe as well as the sugar-loaf hat and the feather-trimmed bonnet. Jeweled neck chains were favorites for both men and women.*

*The feminine version of the houppelande was worn over a richly patterned undergown. High-waisted and belted below the breasts, the houppelande fell into a voluminous trained skirt. Sleeves with fur cuffs were narrow and tight, and fur also frequently made an appearance around the neckline and hem of the gown. Headdresses were extravagant, and among the choices there were the thickly padded escoffion of brocade and jewels; the high, cone-shaped hennin (sometimes three feet in height, the hennin often had a transparent veil attached to the tip, and wires often shaped the veil into beautiful wings); and a horned headgear of two or even three veiled protuberances. Poulaines were of leather or velvet brocade.*

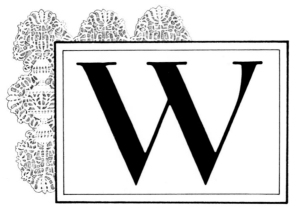

hile the rest of Europe fumbled in the dark, Italy flirted with the light of the Renaissance. Man started to probe into matters that until then had been merely guessed at or glossed over with the superstition that comes of ignorance. During the Middle Ages religion had been a driving force, and while it was still vital (essentially in its artistic aspects), Renaissance man mingled glory to God with a greater glory to his mortal self. As Leonardo da Vinci portrayed the purity and innocence of the Madonna and Child, Pietro Aretino depicted the foibles and licentiousness of mankind. Holiness and bawdiness were not unlikely bedfellows. Indeed, it was the age of earthy enlightenment.

*The human form was conspicuously displayed—particularly in men's clothing. Short tunics scarcely long enough to cover the buttocks were worn over skintight particolored hose. Sometimes—though doubtless* not *for the sake of modesty—a longer, fur-trimmed jerkin or pourpoint was worn. Detachable sleeves were fastened to the tunic at the shoulder with "points"—little metal tags attached to ribbon, string, or leather and used as lacings.* The hair style of the period was of the pageboy type, with thick bangs and smooth shoulder-length hair, turned under at the bottom, crowned with a small velvet cap or beret.*

*The gown of the* nobile donna *was of a relatively simple cut, although the fabrics were luxurious: silk brocades, embroidered satins, and pearl- or gem-strewn velvets. Over the gown was worn a long sleeveless coat, trimmed with fur or jewels and open down the front or at the sides.* Hair was parted in the middle and drawn off the forehead to the nape of the neck, then plaited with ribbon or left to flow freely down the back.* A small gold-embroidered cap and a* ferronière, *a silk cord or fine gold chain with gems worn about the forehead, were musts for every well-dressed Sostrata and Lucrezia.*

"Bulky" is the most fitting term to describe garments worn during the period of Henry VIII's reign. Henry, a tall man, began to widen as he matured, and to camouflage his corpulence his garments were tailored in a stupendous manner; the width of the shoulders was increased and excessive padding was added to the arms and the chest, thus rendering his substantial belly somewhat less obvious. He had well-turned if hefty legs, and the short-skirted doublet enabled him to show them off.

*The fabrics used to create the Tudor look further contributed to its bulky appearance; thick velvet brocades, heavy lustrous satins, often embroidered, and a prodigal share of fur often appeared on a single garment. In addition, by slashing the outer garment and pulling the material of the inner one through the slits, dressmakers achieved an even greater interplay of texture and colors. Even footwear was submitted to techniques of slashing and padding. And on top, a beret-like cap, trimmed with an ostrich plume, was worn at a jaunty angle.*

*The ladies were every bit as "magnyfycent" as the gentlemen. Though the emphasis was not on a wide-shouldered look, an over-all impression of bulk was inescapable. Skirts were voluminous, open in front to display the underskirt or petticoat. The bodice was tight-fitting with a square, often low-cut, jewel-set neckline. Sleeves were also tight, restricting the movement of the arms, and they ended in huge cuffs of a contrasting material or fur. Undersleeves, made of the same fabric as the underskirt, were often slashed and finished in a fine linen or lace ruffle. Feminine millinery was distinctive, to say the least. The gable-peaked hood (worn by Catherine of Aragon and later taken up by Jane Seymour) and the French hood were the most popular styles. The peaked headdress, set with gems and ending in two velvet lappets, enveloped the net-encased hair, and, cumbersome though it may have been, this elegant style managed to impart a demure allure to nearly every face. The French hood, introduced by Anne Boleyn and depicted in many of the younger Holbein portraits, boasted a raised semicircular headband. Studded with pearls or gems, it sat farther back on the head than the gable hood and encased loose, flowing hair in a single velvet lappet that fell to the waist. An excessive amount of jewelry—gold chains, jewel-encrusted brooches, cap ornaments, pendants, and rings (sometimes two or three to a finger)—gave the Tudors the impressive flash that Henry and his court pursued so doggedly.*

Renaissance fashion attained its supreme expression with Elizabeth's ascension to the throne of England. After subduing the turmoil provoked by her half-siblings, Edward and "Bloody" Mary, Elizabeth seized the reins of government and the flowering of Renaissance in England began.

The good and very clever Queen had not been handsomely blest, either physically or temperamentally. She had bad skin, unfortunate teeth, and a miserable disposition; she was sly, stubborn, and vain. Her hair thinned, and eventually there was none of it, so she adopted tightly curled wigs of an intense red-orange hue. Her misuse of make-up to camouflage a poor complexion only made matters worse: paint and powder containing a great deal of lead were thickly applied, and the combination of her stark white complexion, carmine-spotted cheeks, and brilliantined red hair must have bordered on the grotesque. But Elizabeth was fully aware of the image she wished to project. She knew that being the female ruler of one of the most influential powers in the known world would be no easy task and that it was imperative to present herself as a powerful and awesome sovereign. The most visible way to communicate this strength was to dress the part, and this she did.

*English costume became extreme: the petticoat and overskirt of the gown were worn over a huge, drum-shaped hoopskirt, and the bodice was long and pointed, with a very narrow waist. Immense padded sleeves, full and wide at the shoulder and tapering slightly toward the wrist, were finished with deep lace cuffs, while outer decorative sleeves, fixed at the shoulder, were left free to hang and often extended to the ground. A large, elaborately pleated and starched lace ruff framed the head, neck, and bosom, and, as if more emphasis were necessary, wired lace "wings" attached to the back of the shoulders rose from behind the ruff. Over this entire ensemble were attached puffs of fabric, embroideries, gold- and gem-encrusted ornaments, and ropes upon ropes of pearls. (Elizabeth was very fond of pearls and wore as many strands as she could manage.) ❦ White was the color most favored by the Virgin Queen. She was also partial to embroidered fabrics with motifs that pointed out the charms and the symbols of her station. One of her gowns was heavily embroidered with images of eyes and ears, the implication being that she saw and heard everything.*

*Men's costume, on the contrary, became more simplified during the Elizabethan era, and consisted primarily of a shortened doublet, with what was known as a peasecod belly, and full gourd-shaped breeches. The only frosting on the outfit was the frilled or starched lace ruff, though the short cape, often slung over the shoulder, was quite natty and became famous as a tool of chivalry when Sir Walter Raleigh placed his over a puddle of water so that the Queen might cross the cobblestones without soiling her shoes.*

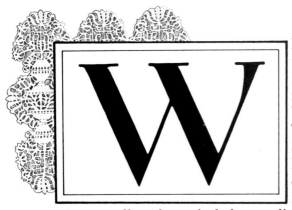

While the Dutch struggled to free themselves from Spain's stranglehold, they nevertheless embraced many elements of fashion favored by their traditional Popish enemy. The mournful colors of severe Spanish costume were quite in keeping with the image of staid dignity and respectability that the Dutch burghers wished to convey. A generally sober-minded, moralistic, and industrious lot, whose instincts for business had made Holland the capital of international finance, the Dutch, however, were not above raising a stein of ale and whooping it up on (rare) occasion.

*Gentlewomen adapted the Spanish* ropa *(or* vlieger, *as we know it today)—a long, unwaisted, and cone-shaped black sleeveless overgown that was open down the front to expose the red underskirt and bodice. The bodice was covered with a richly ornamented stomacher or* borst, *which protruded from the waist and created a particular silhouette.* What originally began as the gathered end of the chemise by now had become a separate item, one that reached millstone proportions, hence the term "millstone ruff." The ruff was often more than four inches thick and composed of regular closed pleats, stiffened with starch to maintain its prim shape, so that a lady's head looked as if it were being offered on a large platter. A starched, lace-edged cap and heavy gold bijouterie *completed the picture of dignity.*

*Gentlemen wore the skirted doublet or jerkin with loose baggy breeches often extending to just below the knees. Twists or wheels of fabric, adapted straight from the Spanish mode, were worn around the shoulders and added breadth to the figure. Unlike the lady's version, the masculine ruff of pleated linen was often left unstarched. The costume was black, but a touch of brilliance was provided by a gaily colored silk sash, tied about the waist or draped over one shoulder.*

After the Spaniards were effectively expelled from Holland their influence on Dutch costume was less pronounced, allowing the French mode to gain the foothold in Holland that it had everywhere else.

**T**he Cavalier period, immortalized in the paintings of Anthony Van Dyck, was an epoch characterized by elegant languor seasoned with a sprig of melancholy. A nobleman cut a dashing figure in his costume of satin and lace, although it is questionable whether he could have accomplished the feats of derring-do that Dumas's Three Musketeers engaged in while dressed in such finery.

*The doublet was more fitted than the corresponding Dutch version; it was belted at the waist and slashed across the chest and often on the sleeves to show off the fine linen skirt worn underneath. Breeches lost their extreme fullness and became longer, ending at or just below the knees. A braid-trimmed satin cape slung over one shoulder gave swagger to the costume, as did the large broad-brimmed hat decorated with ostrich plumes and worn at a rakish angle over the long, flowing hair. Spurred leather boots with large turned-down cuffs, revealing the superb lace of the boot hose, were a trademark of the cavalier.*

*Women's dress retained certain peculiarities of the Elizabethan costume but dismissed a great deal of its exaggeration. The underskirt and the overskirt were still worn, but gone were the immense drum-shaped hoops that held the skirt up and out. Instead, the gown fell in soft, loose folds. The overskirt was often made of a plain material, but the damask petticoat offset the humbleness of the overgarment. The waistline was placed high, and a pregnant look—not unlike the pose adapted during the Middle Ages—emerged. The elaborate Elizabethan ruff became a simple stiffened collar, framing the head, and the collar eventually lost its wiring to fall loosely about the shoulders. Sleeves were full, slashed, or paned, as the cut was then known, from shoulder to waist, then caught up with jeweled ornaments or ribbon to form balloon-like puffs. Through these slits the lining or the undersleeve peeked through, while the wrists were encircled with fine linen or lace cuffs. Softly flowing waves or curls were arranged decoratively on each side of the face, and a braided chignon was customarily worn at the back of the head.*

The Cavalier mode ended in England with the beheading of Charles I. A dapper but unfortunate monarch, he was too much a man and not enough a King. Under the Cromwellian government, fashion took a somber, rather puritanical turn, but with the crowning of Charles II silks and satins, velvets and lace, silver and gold passementerie, ostrich plumes, and countless fripperies were resurrected.

*lé"* lost its punch by the beginning of the seventeenth century, when Spain's obstinate hold on her European conquests went awry. In the sixteenth century Spain had been one of the most powerful and influential countries in the world. Her fashions had infiltrated every European court, including those of her declared enemies. Even Queen Elizabeth turned to the "Spanish mode" for help: the austere elegance, somber colors, and rich, heavy fabrics of Spanish couture expressed a regal dignity that she coveted for herself.

By the time Philip IV took over in 1621, France had become the arbiter of fashion; in contrast to French garb, Spanish apparel seemed way past its prime. Velázquez's court portraits of Philip IV and royal family depict the costume of the period in all its somber glory.

*For the well-bred* señor *fashion prescribed a skirted doublet with prominent shoulder "wings"; double sleeves, the outer one hanging and usually ornamental; and full knee breeches, called "Spanish Slops."* 🪶 *The full neck ruff had been replaced by the* golilla, *a starched semicircular linen collar fitting tightly about the neck.* 🪶 *Large rosettes of ribbon fastened the breeches at the knee, and passementeries and braid were applied with indiscretion, it seems, since these frivolous additions accentuated rather than relieved the stiffness of the costume.*

• *For the* señora: *a large, drum-shaped hoopskirt, the* garde-infanta, *provided a feminine silhouette that was not to be approximated in the fashions of the rest of Europe until the mid-eighteenth century. The garde-infanta was slightly flattened in front and back, and the sides created a width that often equaled the height of the wearer. Over the usually braid-trimmed gown a circular peplum spread out from the waist. The bodice was rigidly corseted and the horizontal neckline topped with a fine linen bertha. Sleeves were puffed and slashed—evocative of the Renaissance—and cuffs of linen frills were fastened at the wrist with ribbons. Jeweled ribbon rosettes also made frequent appearances in the hair and on the bodice.* 🪶 *The coiffure was fashioned in sympathy with the costume's silhouette, and a large hanging plume was often added as an accent.* 🪶 *A large handkerchief was carried—but whether it was ever used is anyone's guess.*

T he male garmenture during this early portion of Louis XIV's seventy-two-year sway (1643–1715) was unequivocally prissy.

*The most striking features of the frothy ensemble were the "petticoat breeches," composed of a full, gathered skirt, either divided for each leg or left as a single piece. Ending at the knee and finished with deep lace flounces and loops of ribbon, the breeches undoubtedly denied comfort but they more than made up for it all in flamboyance. ❧ The coat fitted snugly across the shoulders and was of either bolero or knee length. The sleeves of the coat had moderate turned-back cuffs, all the better to show off the lace and ribbon-festooned silk shirt sleeves. ❧ A lace jabot dribbled down the shirt front, a pleated lace cravat hugged the neck, and ribbons, buttons, and braid contributed further to the litter. ❧ Shoes were high-heeled, square-toed affairs, fastened with starched, lace-trimmed bows that were studded with jeweled ornaments. ❧ As if all this were not enough, a baldric was worn across the chest. Often fringed and embroidered, it ended in loops of ribbon encasing the hilt of the sword that it carried. ❧ The full-bottomed wig was distinguished by rows upon rows of sausage-like curls or was left in a natural, frizzy mass. ❧ The* pièce de resistance, *however, was indubitably the* chapeau. *Low-crowned with an ample brim, it had a glorious froth of ribbon loops and ostrich plumes. Ribbon seems to have been the only element that gave the costume some consistency.*

*The costume of the fair sex had its generous share of laces and ribbons, but all in all it was slightly more harmonious. Over an embroidered satin or taffeta petticoat the velvet overskirt was looped back and held by ribbon rosettes. The matching bodice was dotted with jeweled clasps, buttons, or bowknots of graduated size. The décolletage was edged with a lace or fine lingerie scarf, and the lingerie sleeves were garnished with lace ruffles and ribbon loops. ❧ Hair was puffed out on either side of the face with dangling curls; a chignon glamorized the back of the head, and curly bangs fringed the forehead. ❧ High-heeled slippers, elbow-length gloves, and the ever-prevalent fan were, of course,* de rigueur.

It has been said that Louis XIV was the epitome of kingliness; no one would doubt that his court boasted a lion's share of razzle-dazzle.

oward the end of the Sun King's reign, an early version of today's three-piece suit—matching coat, waistcoat or vest, and knee breeches—presented itself. With slight variations in length and cut of the coat and vest, size of the sleeve cuff, flare of the coat's skirt, and fit of the breeches, the costume retained its basic shape until the French Revolution.

*During this period the coat or* justaucorp *became more neatly tailored, being fitted at the waist, with deep pleats in the back that formed a flared skirt. The sleeves ended in oversize turned-backed cuffs, which sometimes extended as far back as the elbow. The waistcoat, which was often sleeveless, was slightly shorter than the justaucorp, ending just above the knee. Both justaucorp and waistcoat were trimmed brilliantly with embroidery, gold or silver braids (known as brandenburgs), and jewel-studded buttons. The breeches also ended at the knee, and the stockings were either rolled above them or tucked under them. High red-heeled shoes with gold, silver, or jeweled buckles were much in fashion, but the real show-stopper was the peruke. A true work of art, this elaborate wig was in effect a mound consisting of two wavy peaks that gently cascaded over the head and shoulders in thick, soft curls, ending at the waist in back and at mid-chest in front. The coiffure was so luxuriant that the hat was more often carried than worn so that the undulating locks would not be disturbed.*

*Women's habiliment was the very acme of Baroque ornamentation. The overskirt, pulled back from the waist and draped over the hips to create a bustlelike effect, fell into a lengthy train. The extravagant petticoat, which draped in symmetrical folds, was festooned with braid, fringe, appliqué work, and lace (sometimes all on the same garment). The bodice, often made of the same fabric as the overskirt, had a low, square décolletage and elbow-length sleeves ending in multiple lace ruffles. Ladies' headpieces, though not as enormous as the men's, were no less elaborate. A triple tier of lace and ribbon—the* fontage—*often rose two feet or more from the top of the head and was tilted slightly forward. (Rumor has it that the Duchesse de Fontage, while riding during the hunt, stopped to bind up her disheveled coiffure with her beribboned lace garter. The king admired the effect, and the style galloped into legend.) Beauty patches, or* mouches, *were all the rage and continued to be well into the eighteenth century. These patches of gummed taffeta were imbued with significant meanings depending on where they were placed—the bosom or face—but more often than not they camouflaged a multitude of epidermal imperfections.*

ouis XIV breathed his last in 1715—and most of France heaved a sigh of relief. The Sun King had reigned for nearly three-quarters of a century, and though he had brought great glory to France, the pomp and circumstance attending his court had eventually become old hat. As the Baroque era passed, the Regency style began to germinate, but this was just the beginning of the glorious Rococo bloom. The Regency brought with it a new freshness and freedom in fashion and morals alike. Philippe, the Duc d'Orleans, was an intelligent, diligent regent, and he possessed a soft spot for the ladies. During his rule women began to achieve a position of influence (notoriety as well) that has not been equaled until the present day. When Louis XV came of age and took over the reins of government, the ladies were in their heyday—and so was Louis. His stint on the throne became known as the Petticoat Reign. After a succession of minor mistresses and a rather lukewarm marriage, he settled down with Madame de Pompadour.

The cultivated Madame de Pompadour ruled Louis and, through him, France. A woman of taste, she dabbled in a bit of everything artistic and, with disastrous results, political. The Louis XV style should have been known as the Style Pompadour, for Madame nurtured the delicate, ribbon-entwined, flower-garlanded, porcelained, and pastel-colored world of the Rococo.

*Women's costume reached an apex of feminine luxury. The* pannier *or hooped skirt was worn under an exquisite gown of patterned silk, ribbon, and lace. Dome-shaped, the pannier eventually flattened out front and back and extended laterally, reaching its greatest breadth during the following reign. A must it was for every* grande toilette. *The* robe à la française, *or gown, was open down the front to reveal the matching underskirt. Box pleats attached to the neckline flowed into a graceful train. Sleeves were narrow and of elbow length, ending in* engageantes, *a froth of lace and ribbon. The bodice was trimmed with ribbon loops of graduated size and the décolletage finished with a frill of lace.* ❧ *The* coiffure, *at first dressed close to the head and powdered white, later rose and by the 1770s became a veritable tower.*

*Men's costume retained the Baroque "three-piece suit" but it was now designated the* habit à la française. *Other than a sloping away from the front and a reduction in the fullness of the coat skirt, sleeve cuffs, and breeches, gentlemen's apparel altered little.* ❧ *The wig lost its fullness, and a series of curls dressed close to the head ended in a black-silk-encased queue.*

I t was the best of times, it was the worst of times . . . there were a king with a large jaw and a queen with a plain face, on the throne of England; there were a king with a large jaw and a queen with a fair face, on the throne of France." So observed Charles Dickens in *A Tale of Two Cities*. The reigns of George III and Louis XVI began full of promise; they ended full of fury. Obstinate George lost his American colonies and his mind; dull-witted Louis was relieved of his throne and his head. The eighteenth century became known as the Age of Enlightenment, but the ill-starred monarchs were far less in the know than their inquisitive subjects. Common man scrutinized the privileges of aristocracy, and the consequences of the investigation were not very pretty.

Marie Antoinette, Queen of France, arbiter of fashion, grande dame of elegant extravagance, set the stylish trends and was slavishly copied not only at Versailles but at royal courts throughout Europe. With Marie Antoinette at the helm, fashions changed daily: one day's whim was the next day's passé fancy. Capricious and self-indulgent, she whiled away her evenings at risqué masked Opera Balls or in disreputable gambling dens, and by the light of day she closeted herself with Rose Bertin, couturière, or with Monsieur Leonard, coiffeur.

*For full dress* (de rigueur *at court functions), elaborate silk gowns were worn over immense panniers. Generously bestowed with festoons of lace, puffs of fabric, artificial flowers, jewels, and ribbons, the gowns were so wide that ladies had to pass through doors sideways. When they traveled, the doors of their sedan chairs or carriages were often left open to allow the gown to extend outside the vehicle.* 🪭 *As gowns widened, coiffeurs heightened. Hair was brushed up from the forehead and festooned with false puffs, curls, and braids, and then pomaded and powdered. Hairdos sometimes towered a full three feet.* 🪭 *A lace-trimmed bonnet, strands of pearls or diamonds, flowers, and a panache of plumes were added to boot.*

*For everyday frolics, the ladies chose a calf-length gown worn over a smaller hoop. One of the more treasured versions was the* robe à la polonaise, *a short dress with an overskirt draped in three large swags, the fullness controlled by cords attached at the waist. Colorful hand-painted or block-printed cotton from the East—known as* indiennes—*was the fabric of choice.* 🪭 *Fans, walking sticks, parasols, gloves, and small bouquets of flowers worn at the bosom were vital accoutrements.*

# Rococo/Neoclassic—Louis XVI and Marie Antoinette, 1780–1790

The 1780s introduced a bucolic thread to high-fashion stitchery. Panniers became passé, elaborate trimmings were considered too froufrou, and towering hair styles suddenly brought on migraines. Jean-Jacques Rousseau beckoned for a "return to nature" and the Queen, bored with the doldrums of court life and its rigorous etiquette, subscribed to a more relaxed and rustic life. In admiration of English simplicity, clothing took on an informal tone. The ladies literally and figuratively let down their hair.

Marie Antoinette established a cozy retreat at the Petit Trianon. There she had built, for her amusement, a *hameau* (hamlet) in the "rustic style." The artificial village was equipped with a water-wheel mill, a dairy, cottages for the carefully scrubbed peasants, and a barn for the gorgeously groomed gilt-hooved cattle. The hamlet was a study in cultivated theatricality: at first it appeared quaintly dilapidated, but closer inspection revealed that the cracks and patina of age had been painted onto the walls and doors. Here Marie Antoinette, dressed simply in the style known as the *chemise à la reine,* played at farming.

*The chemise, a sheer cotton or light silk frock, was deeply ruffled around the décolletage and tied at the waist with a wide, soft sash. A large Leghorn hat, enriched with ribbon and ostrich plumes, and a shepherdess crook consummated the ensemble.*

The mania for garments in the English style supposedly arrived in France from Great Britain with the introduction of horseracing. The elegant and seemingly unstudied simplicity of the clothing worn by the British gentry's horsey set appealed to the frivolous French. The influence may have been British, but the total effect was undoubtably French.

*The gown* à la Levite *was based on the Englishwoman's redingote, a long double-breasted coat, with turndown collar and a shoulder cape. The Levite gown had a double-breasted jacket with wide lapels, fitted sleeves, and a small shoulder cape. Worn with a trained gown and a fine linen jabot, it was considered very much the* style anglaise. *The oversized hat of dotted gauze was finished with a spray of artificial flowers and two jaunty ostrich plumes. Watch fobs at the waist and a carved walking stick gave the outfit a decidedly mannish look.*

The thunderclouds of discontent swelled and then burst, releasing the torrential French Revolution and the Reign of Terror. Suddenly the elite had more important things to think about than what was or was not à la mode.

obespierre, "the incorruptible," was delivered to the guillotine in 1794. Without a moment to spare (save for a splendid little bit of merry-making), France began piecing together the remnants of government into some semblance of order. The Reign of Terror was bloody well over, and the miasma of anxiety gave way to frenzied high spirits and nonchalance.

Release from the extravagant powdered wigs, over-bedizened hoopskirts, and silk-embroidered *habit à la française* of the Ancien Regime took the form of exaggerated trumpery.

*Garments* à la grecque *or in the "antique" style were all the rage. A citizeness wouldn't think of appearing in anything but a long flowing gown ending in a train that was often carried over the arm; a high waistline; and a scandalously low neckline.* ❧ *A draped shawl of cashmere or lace was an imperative sideline.* ❧ *Hats or bonnets were large-brimmed coal-skuttle affairs or oversize loops of ribbon attached to a ruffle of dangling lace.* ❧ Les merveilleuses *(or "marvelous ones," as the ladies were called) developed exaggerated poses and bizarre movements to show off their finery. They believed that the attitudes they assumed were in keeping with the "antique" style.*

*Their male counterparts,* les incroyables *("the incredibles"), were as fanatical about their dress as the ladies were. High, turned-down collars and huge lapels on tight-fitting coats, two or three mismatched vests, form-revealing breeches (that eventually evolved into even more incommodious trousers), and huge neckcloths that sometimes swathed the face as well as the neck completed the dandy look.* ❧ *Gentlemen carried heavy knotted walking sticks and wore large tricorne hats fancied up with ribbon cockades as an extra measure of dash.*

With the rise of Napoleon, this sartorial splendor was diluted and then jelled into what became the Empire Style.

**T**he roll of drums and the rattle of sabers reverberated throughout the royal courts and embassies of Europe, the Middle East, and Asia as Napoleon Bonaparte retrieved the crown of France from the mud into which it had fallen and placed it firmly on his brow. During his administration, war and war talk were rampant. Napoleon had managed to upset most of the ruling classes of Europe and even succeeded in placing his own kin on the thrones of some of them. His ambition was to restore the prestige and power that France once knew—before the Bourbons had bungled and the revolution had further muddled. He established an Imperial court and upheld ancient Rome as the prototype for his own Empire. The classic prevailed in all things artistic, including *haute couture.*

*For the imperial dame: a high-waisted gown, predominantly white, often with embroidery in gold threads or colored silks. If the (detachable) sleeves were not worn, extremely long embroidered gloves took their place. ❧ For court habiliment, a richly decorated train—a* courrobe—*of velvet or satin and of a different color from the dress itself was attached to the bodice just below the bust. ❧ A wired lace collar reminiscent of the sixteenth century—referred to as a Medici collar—framed the bust, neck, and head. It also served as a perfect foil for the heavily jeweled necklaces, earrings, and tiaras. ❧ Flat-soled slippers, sometimes embroidered and set with gems, framed dainty feet. ❧ Shawls were often draped around the shoulders to accentuate a graceful pose.*

*Gentlemen's attire remained much as it had during the Directoire period, but exaggerated details were done away with. Lapels and collars attained a normal width and position on the coat, which itself became more fitted. ❧ Tight knee-breeches were still worn but ultimately evolved into long trousers. ❧ The martial theme was dominant, and uniforms, colorful and diverse, were in order. The uniforms were dashingly cut and fitted, lavishly braid- and button-trimmed, and worn with a fur-edged outer jacket which was slung over one shoulder. ❧ Tall, highly polished boots and extravagantly embellished headgear were the ultimate regalia.*

With the end of the Napoleonic Era, a sorry Europe sobered up and put itself aright. New developments, economic, political, and scientific, introduced themselves and men ruminated on topics quite divorced from the subject of fashion.

The Romantic era was a period of exaggerated, often affected sensibility. Women were apt to take alarm or to swoon at any provocation; men displayed a nonchalance and bravado that often masked their genuine inclinations. The rosy-colored scene: A delicate feminine profile intently bows over an embroidery frame, her pale features illuminated by the light of a glass-globed oil lamp. By her side a young beau languidly turns the pages of a small leather-bound volume and murmurs the studied verse, which bespeaks a deep and self-sacrificing love.

During the 1830s a treasure trove of historical periods was resurrected and a revival, which was to continue through the remainder of the century, was aswing. The Gothic period, for one, received a thorough going over; many of its architectural motifs were applied faithfully or stylized to fit the romantic idea of the Middle Ages. Vast cathedrals and seaside cottages alike were built with their share of trefoil piercings, arched doorways, and stained-glass windows. The Renaissance was also summoned for inspiration, and female costume bore the brunt of the pickings.

*Sleeves were large, puffed, and slashed; the broad-shouldered look was back. During the end of the 1820s and well into the 30s, sleeves reached monstrous proportions. At first the fullness was at the top of the sleeve, which tapered to a close fit at the wrist. The leg-of-mutton or* gigot *sleeve was stuffed with down cushions and supported by flexible whale boning. Later, the fullness dropped to the elbow and was caught in puffs from there to the wrist. The sleeve itself was set halfway down the upper arm, confining arm movement and producing a broad, sloping shoulder line. This was further exaggerated by a large and wide falling collar, capelet, or bertha, that created a "roof" over the shoulders and arms. Waists were tightly laced, and ankle-length skirts became full and bell-shaped. Seven or eight petticoats were often worn to add width. The broadened torso, wasp waist, and full skirt provided a sassy hour-glass silhouette. The fragile doll-like appearance was further heightened by a face-framing bonnet of shirred fabric or straw, flower- and ribbon-trimmed, and by square-toed, flat-heeled slippers tied about the ankle.*

*The Romantic dude's costume echoed the feminine silhouette in its sloping broad shoulder line and low-set padded sleeves. The shawl collar of the frock coat swelled over the chest, then curved back from the waist. (Tight corseting insured a modish look.) The coat then fell over the hips and ended in tails at the back. Trousers were well-fitted and held taut by a strap under the instep. Narrow, square-toed leather boots, a gold-pommeled walking stick, and a high-crowned top hat were indispensable adjuncts for the well-dressed dandy.*

# Victorian Era (the Crinoline), 1850–1870

The mid-nineteenth century found Queen Victoria sober, dowdy, ultraethical, and seated on the English throne. With the able assistance of her adored mate, Prince Albert of Saxe-Coburg, she kept close watch over her large litter of kin and her even larger empire. In France, meanwhile, the debonair Emperor Napoleon III and his beautiful consort, Eugénie de Montijo, presided over what appeared to be one huge, never-ending soirée. It was an era of the parvenu and everyone was out to have a rollicking time. Extravagance was unrivaled; taste was questionable. It was also the period of the pastiche in art, architecture, decoration, and costume, and elements from a host of historical periods were rounded up and mixed and matched with abandon. The result was a potpourri of styles that contributed in no small measure to the vulgar opulence that earmarked the Second Empire.

*The crinoline (hooped skirt) replaced the plethora of petticoats that stuffed the fashions of the previous period. Lighter and not as hampering, the crinoline nonetheless created an even greater swelling of the skirt. The width of the gown sometimes reached a flabbergasting circumference of eighteen feet.*

The Second Empire also gave rise to the House of Worth. If Napoleon III was Emperor of the French, Charles Frederick Worth was the undisputed Sovereign of Fashion. Pampered American heiresses, staid English peeresses, and all the moneyed demimonde of Paris flocked to Worth's salon. Every fashionable woman coveted a gown bearing the Worth label. And what gowns they were! Over the vast crinolines were worn creations of silk, satin, velvet, or taffeta, patched with puffs of tulle, festooned with garlands of flowers, flounced with ruffles of ribbons and lace, and sprinkled with gems. Worth's ball gowns were flights of fantasy, reminiscent of Marie Antoinette and her dapper court. His daytime ensembles were models of originality and sumptuous craftsmanship.

*For excursions into the country—a favored pastime—a shorter, less restrictive gown was chosen. For croquet and leisurely hikes culminating in a lunch al fresco, women took to a mid-calf- or ankle-length dress with a draped overskirt. The overskirt, often of a different color and material from that of the dress, matched the fitted jacket. Plaids and stripes were "in" and colors vibrant. ※ Ankle-high* bottines *were high-heeled and buttoned, revealing a well-turned calf and regarded as quite daring and provocative. The empress hat, decorated with curled ostrich plumes, was favored by Eugénie.*

*Gentlemen's apparel was also modified to adapt well to the leisurely ambiance. A tailed frock coat with embroidered vest and a top hat would be totally impractical for traipsing through the woods, so "sports clothes" found an eager audience. The knee-length "knicker" suit in checkered wool with matching cap and sturdy shoes could be worn for hunting and traveling and for indulging in an assortment of outdoor amusements.*

# Victorian Era (the Bustle), 1870–1890

**N**ever before in the history of costume had fabric suffered such abuse in the name of fashion. Yards of it were swagged, bunched, puffed, pleated, and draped into bizarre configurations. During the late 1860s the crinoline shed its dome shape and assumed a conical form; the front was flattened and the rear emphasized. The fabric was bunched high over a padded roll of stiffened horsehair flounce that was placed just below the waist in the back. Eventually the bum-roll became the whalebone-and-horsehair structure known as the *tournure* or bustle.

During the 1870s the bustle did impart a certain charm and dignity to the wearer. The ladies, with puffs, swags, and sweeping trains, emulated exotically colored birds with trailing plumage. The bustle disappeared in the middle of the decade, leaving the accumulated puffs and flounces of the gown to sweep languidly across the floor, without benefit of support. In the 80s, however, the bustle suddenly reappeared in a thoroughly grotesque form: jutting out sharply from the waist, it exaggerated the posterior to such an extent that one might have wondered what kind of hideous growths were being camouflaged.

*For proper daytime dressing, the bodice of the gown was tight-fitting, high-necked, and buttoned down the front. It was topped with a small lace ruff, and its long sleeves, often finished in a turned-back cuff, exposed the lace-edged sleeve of the blouse worn beneath it. For evening, the neckline of the sleeveless gown was cut low and the gown was worn off the shoulder, thus revealing a great deal of bosom and bare arm. Multicolored fabrics of two or three different textures were sometimes used for a single ensemble. This variety of color and texture and the excessive fussiness of the trimmings gave the onlooker the impression that perhaps designers were not quite sure what they were doing. A lady would not dare to sally forth without her beloved parasol walking stick.*

The eighteenth century was resurrected and rather overworked in the 1860s and 70s. Articles of apparel, no matter how far removed they were from the Rococo, were styled à la Pompadour, à la Trianon, or à la Marie Antoinette. The coiffure, for instance, elaborately dressed and crowned with a flower-, feather-, and ribbon-trimmed hat, was considered to be styled in the eighteenth-century mode.

*Men's costume (in which to conduct business, visit the racetrack, or attend a daytime wedding) consisted of the frock coat, vest, and trousers. The frock coat retained its tails, but it was of a more generous cut. Trousers were baggy and generally fashioned from striped material. A dark-colored vest with a gold watch chain draped across its expanse was inevitably donned, and no fashionable gentleman would be without his top hat, walking stick, and gloves.*

42

dward VII—head of state, sports enthusiast, womanizer—was the quintessential bon vivant of the late nineteenth and early twentieth centuries. He appreciated a full-fleshed and rather playful feminine type, and, what with the Edwardian manner of extravagant dining, the ladies had but little leeway in the matter of weight control. As for their coquettish manner, their spiffy undergarments contributed to that. As much time, money, and workmanship were spent on petticoats and bloomers as on the gowns concealing them. Their seductive presence, however, was announced by the distinct rustle of petticoat silk, or glimpsed when the skirt was raised as a lady entered or exited from a carriage. "A whole world of meaning could be conveyed by the way the dress was held up, from a prudish snub to the most daring flirtatiousness." (H. H. Hansen.)

*A superfluous assortment of silk flounces, lace, appliqué, and ribbon titivated the gown as well as the unmentionables. The dress, high-necked during the day, was cut daringly low for the evening. The high collar of lace and embroidery was stiffened with bone and often formed a biblike covering on the bodice. The bosom was entrusted to a loose blouse which hung pouchlike to just below the waistline in front. Sleeves were long or elbow-length, in which case gloves were worn day or night. The trumpet-shaped skirt was fitted over the hips, then flared toward the hem, and ended in a train. Tight corseting was the rule of the day, and the figure was formed into a pronounced sway-backed "S" shape. The corset shifted the emphasis of the figure forward into the bust and backward behind the hips. Delicious hats were as profusely decorated as the gowns, and no outfit could be complete without a matching parasol.*

*Men's clothing became noticeably more casual. The blue blazer, white flannels, and straw boater were a far cry from the feather-trimmed tricorne and satin court attire of the 1770s and the vested morning suit of the 1870s. This laid-back costume has, with variation in cut and fit, remained much the same up to the present day.*

When King Edward died in 1910, a whole way of life passed on with him. Royal personages and heads of state from every country and principality in Europe gathered to pay homage, but little did they know that they were witnessing their own last rites as well. In five years' time the First World War would rearrange the face of Europe and eliminate, for a majority of the rulers present, their thrones and their *raison d'être.*

aul Poiret, *"enfant terrible* of the Paris fashion world," did wonders for the feminine silhouette. By designing gowns on simple vertical lines, he revolutionized the whole concept of dress. Superfluous frills, flounces, pleats, tucks, and the restrictive "S"-bend corset were taboo. Out went rustling lace-trimmed petticoats; in came simple tubelike tunics, belted just below the breasts à la Empire. Eventually the dress narrowed toward the hem and the "hobble skirt" was born. From the knees to the ankles the legs were constricted, and though a slit at the side or at the front of the sheath alleviated the narrow situation somewhat, mobility was reduced to a mincing gait. Trousers for women were considered scandalous; Poiret adored them and introduced the "harem" or "trouser" skirt. The harem skirt was either a skirt separated at the knees or baggy, ankle-length trousers. For evening wear it was half hidden by an overdress left open at the sides or in front. Poiret's "lampshade" tunic could also top the harem skirt. A belted knee-length tunic with a wired hem that flared out over the slim figure, it was known also as the "minaret dress." The Ballets Russes and their brilliant use of design and color inspired the Sultan of Fashion to take up with his own palette of vibrant primary colors. The Oriental flavor of Ballets Russes productions inspired him yet further—he developed the "kimono style" and the turban.

*For a gala opera or concert performance, ladies wore a draped, narrow-hemmed skirt, ending in a "mermaid train," under a slit-fronted sheath. A kimono-style evening wrap of black velvet trimmed with white fox was embellished with beadwork and with a set of hanging tassels at the back. Strands of pearls decorated the plumed turban, and beadwork made up the stylized peacock-feather design on the overskirt.*

*Gentlemen's apparel was sober in comparison. Elegance was evident only in the cut and fit of the clothes. No dramatic effects were at play. Suits were dark colored, and for evening black was required. The tailcoat, white vest, bow tie, and gloves were staples in every fashionable wardrobe.*

With the coming of war, fashion took a back seat to far more pertinent issues. There wasn't time or energy or money to indulge in the world of fashion, which is not to say that design and style were not evident in women's clothes during those bitter years. Fashion was simply not as important as it had been.